MASTER PLAN

A Community Association Strategic Planning Guide for Homeowners Associations, Condominiums, and Housing Cooperatives

ALAN ROBBINS

Copyright © 2020 Alan Robbins
All rights reserved
First Edition

PAGE PUBLISHING, INC.
Conneaut Lake, PA

First originally published by Page Publishing 2020

ISBN 978-1-64701-232-8 (pbk)
ISBN 978-1-64701-234-2 (hc)
ISBN 978-1-64701-233-5 (digital)

Printed in the United States of America

To Maureen—my deepest gratitude for your love, support, and infinite patience… Your devotion and willingness to always be there for family, friends, and community sets an example that we should all follow.

CONTENTS

DUST ON THE PAGES 7
INTRODUCTION 9
PROLOGUE: FOREST GROVE…2011 13

**CHAPTER I: COMMUNITY ASSOCIATION
                BASICS AND THE FOUDATION FOR
                PLANNING** 17
- ❖ The Role of the Community Association 18
- ❖ Planning Leadership 20
- ❖ Is It Time to Move Ahead? 22

**CHAPTER II: THE THREE-PHASE PLANNING
                PROCESS** 23
- ❖ Strategic Planning Fundamentals 24
- ❖ The CAPSERV Strategic Planning Process 24
- ❖ Phase 1: Preplanning Session:
  Preparation and Research 25
- ❖ Planning Facilitator's
  Preparation and Research Checklist 26
- ❖ Phase 2: The Planning Session:
  Plan Development 28
- ❖ Phase 3: Postplanning Session:
  Plan Implementation 31
- ❖ Gauging Your Association's Success 32
- ❖ Linking the Budget to the Plan 34

CHAPTER III: EFFECTIVE COMMUNICATION AND SURVEYS 35
- ❖ The Need for Proactive Communication 36
- ❖ Consensus Building and Managing Expectations 37
- ❖ Effective Surveys 38
- ❖ Data Review and SWOT Analysis 40
- ❖ Survey Process Management 42

CHAPTER IV: THE CAPSERV SIX-POINT STRATEGIC PLAN MODEL 44
- ❖ The Model 45
- ❖ The Vision Statement 46
- ❖ The Mission Statement 46
- ❖ Strengths, Weaknesses, Opportunities, and Threats ... 46
- ❖ Goals, Strategies, and Action Steps 47
- ❖ Communications and Feedback 47
- ❖ Plan Review and Modification 47

ADDENDUM A: THE 2011 FOREST GROVE COMMUNITY SURVEY 49
ADDENDUM B: THE 2011 SURVEY RESULTS AND SWOT ANALYSIS 57
ADDENDUM C: THE 2011 FOREST GROVE STRATEGIC PLAN 66

EPILOGUE: FOREST GROVE…2014 93
REFERENCES 97
ABOUT THE AUTHOR 100

DUST ON THE PAGES

Why do so many strategic plans fail? All too often, a lack of understanding about the wants and needs of the community, poor communication, unrealistic goals, and a lack of emphasis on implementation lead to failure. The end result...plans written with the best of intentions and lofty ideas end up being set aside on shelves, to be forgotten and do nothing more than gather dust on their pages.

Successful planning fosters proactive communication, a deep understanding of a plan's mission and goals, and a greater sense of ownership of the plan within the community. The **CAPSERV** Strategic Planning Process featured in this book is a guide for the development of a plan that can serve as a road map to success. It outlines research that should be conducted prior to plan development, how to conduct the planning session, the components of a well-written plan, and how to properly implement and execute the plan after it is written.

I am a believer in in the power of well-thought-out strategic plans supported by proactive communication and purposeful implementation. They are the foundation for work that can be done to create communities that we can all be proud to call home.

—Alan Robbins

INTRODUCTION

When I meet with community association boards about strategic planning, I am usually asked two questions. The first is, "Why did our past planning efforts fail?" The second is, "What differentiates your strategic plans from other plans?"

The answers to the first question can be very complex. Many plans fail because of inadequate planning preparation, poor communication, a lack of leadership during the planning process, failure to reach out to the community to determine what homeowners really want or need, and an inability to motivate the volunteers who will have to carry out plan initiatives. These problems are often compounded after planning is completed, when plans are not effectively implemented and work is not properly monitored to ensure that objectives are met in a timely and cost-effective manner.

The answers to the second question are relatively simple. The strategic plan template that I use isn't much different than other templates that can easily be found on the Internet. The real difference is the **CAPSERV** Strategic Planning Process. This process enables community associations to avoid the pitfalls that cause so many plans to fail. **CAPSERV** is a formal process that organizes planning functions into three distinct phases. During the first phase, advance preparation work is done and research is conducted to make certain that planning session participants know what is expected of them, that they understand the expected outcomes of the planning session, and that they have information about the association and community that they will need to develop a viable plan. In the second phase, a planning session is held that is structured to enable participants to stay on task with enough time to thoroughly develop the plan's goals and the strategies required to achieve those goals. During the third and final phase, after the strategic plan has been written and approved by the board of directors, association volunteers are given the opportunity to establish and implement action steps required to carry out the plan's various strategies. Work is closely monitored with sufficient board oversight to ensure timely completion of plan initiatives within the framework of the association's budget.

CAPSERV simplifies the process and emphasizes an important factor that many planners overlook…a practical, common-sense approach that reinforces the benefits of sound planning leadership, effective communication, and the need to promote the planning agenda at all times in order to ensure the support of the volunteer base and community.

This book is about Forest Grove, a fictional community that is based upon a composite of communities and associations that I have worked with over the years. The association's day-to-day operations were relatively well managed, but in a changing world, the board of directors was losing touch with the general membership, the association was struggling to maintain the original vision for the community, and Forest Grove was no longer meeting homeowner expectations. Despite earnest attempts, the board had been unable to develop an effective, long-term strategic plan. Beginning in this book's prologue and ending with its epilogue, you will read about how **CAPSERV** planning solutions were used to develop and implement a successful plan that proactively changed the course of the community's future.

Addenda A, B, and C are devoted to Forest Grove's community wide survey, the survey's results, and the strategic plan that was developed following the **CAPSERV** approach. These examples can be used as working models as you develop your own plan. It is my hope that by connecting Forest Grove's story with the **CAPSERV** planning process, your association volunteers will gain a deeper understanding about how to develop and execute a plan that will bring great value to your community.

Forest Grove is a fictional community that is based on a composite of communities that I have worked with over the years. Any resemblance in this book to those communities or their associations is unintended and entirely coincidental.

PROLOGUE

FOREST GROVE...2011

In May 2011, I received a call from the president of the Forest Grove Community Association to discuss strategic planning. Forest Grove was developed in suburban Bethesda, Maryland, during the mid 1980s. The community consisted of 624 single-family detached homes. Amenities included a centrally located two-story clubhouse and exercise center, swimming pool, children's playground, adjacent parking lots, extensive open green space, and a network of asphalt walking paths that meandered through the community's densely wooded common areas.

Members of the board were concerned that the community was slipping away from its original design concept. This problem was being driven by covenant violations that had been increasing at a problematic rate over the past few years. Questions had been raised about the adequacy of the association's operating budget, and it was unclear as to whether enough reserve funds were available to cover needed infrastructure repair and replacement work. These concerns were compounded by a rising level of complaints from homeowners about the community's aging appearance.

We spent some time discussing my planning process and agreed that I would meet with the board. At my request, the president had copies of the association's governing documents, policies, budget, and latest reserve study delivered to me for review prior to the meeting. I also received copies of the developer's original sales brochures. This marketing material was very helpful since it provided a comprehensive description of the original concept for the development. Forest Grove was intended to be a peaceful and tranquil place, far from the hustle and bustle of Bethesda's urban business district. Photographs of the clubhouse and brick, stone, and wood homes nestled among the trees created an image of a neighborhood that would blend in with the natural beauty of the surrounding area. It was all there…a complete picture of the timeless vision for a community that could be preserved for years to come.

I arrived early so that I could look around and form my own opinion about the issues that were concerning the board. As I approached my destination, I couldn't help but notice that civilization had caught up with the community. Local roadways were dotted with trendy shopping centers and office buildings. The construction boom was well underway. New residential communities with impressive entrances, heavily landscaped roadways, wide arrays of amenities, and the latest, up-to-date housing styles were popping up everywhere. These new developments were bound to have an impact on prospective homebuyers and the resale value of older homes in the area.

Forest Grove's homes, situated on generously sized lots, lined curved roadways. Mature elm and oak trees that had been planted in the front of each lot by the developer added nicely to the area's wooded appearance. Unfortunately, there were signs that the community had, indeed, begun to drift away from its original design concept. While the majority of homes continued to follow the earthen-tone color palate established by the developer, there was a fair amount of homes with trim, shutters, and doors that were painted with bright primary or lighter pastel colors, causing them to stand out rather than blend in with the surrounding woodlands. While most homes were well-kept and attractive, the streetscapes were marred by poorly maintained homes with lawns that were not regularly mowed and landscape beds overgrown with weeds and dead or dying bushes.

MASTER PLAN

The exterior of the clubhouse and exercise center, located in a traditional brick building, was attractive and in good condition, but the building's interior paint, carpeting, furniture, and decorations were worn and outdated. While the swimming pool, pool deck, and playground equipment appeared to be well maintained, the adjacent asphalt parking lot had been neglected. Its surface was marred with cracks and dips that presented serious tripping hazards. Private asphalt roads and walking paths were also in need of extensive repairs. Landscaping in common areas was weak and well below acceptable standards for the price points of the community's homes. Entry features were not as attractive or appealing as other communities in the general area.

Forest Grove had excellent potential; however, it was evident that the association had failed to systematically address its long-term infrastructure needs. The volunteer effort and cost to address these problems would be high… I looked forward to an interesting meeting with the board.

CHAPTER I

COMMUNITY ASSOCIATION BASICS AND THE FOUDATION FOR PLANNING

FOREST GROVE...A FRANK AND MEANINGFUL DISCUSSION

As my discussion with the board and managing agent began, we agreed that my first impressions of the community's strengths and weaknesses were accurate. It was evident that there was a consensus amongst the directors about the need for a major planning initiative, but there was also a good deal of frustration about past failures and a lack of confidence about their ability to put together a viable plan that would actually work. In the past, the board constantly ran into roadblocks that interfered with its ability to get the job done. Committee volunteers were not engaged and continued to focus on their own objectives and "pet" projects. Internal politics and squabbling among the committees about implementation authority and responsibilities often dominated productive discussion. Most notably, there was little homeowner "buy-in," or interest in what the board was attempting to do. While most day-to-day operations were in order, the board, committee volunteers, and managing agent appeared to be "lost in the weeds" when it came to dealing with the community's long-term needs.

After listening to the group for an hour, it was evident that their difficulties centered on a lack of clear understanding about the strategic planning process and the need for strong planning leadership. I took some time to review the history and benefits of community associations and why this lifestyle concept was so successful. I then moved on to an overview of the different types of associations and their common core responsibilities. We discussed the need for strong planning leadership and a common-sense approach to clear communications, concise direction, and a willingness to motivate the volunteer base during the planning process. The board members unanimously agreed that they were ready for change and that it was time to move ahead.

THE ROLE OF THE COMMUNITY ASSOCIATION

In the 1960s, migration from urban city centers to the suburbs led to the beginning of the modern community association movement. A willingness on the part of municipalities and counties to allow real estate developers to increase land density and the availability of a growing number of low-cost funding sources encouraged large-scale residential development. Developers began to understand that communities with shared amenities would attract potential homebuyers. Homeowners who resided in neighborhoods governed by community associations appreciated the benefits of collective management that protected their property rights. They also learned that sharing expenses with their neighbors for maintenance and upkeep of their community's common areas and amenities enabled them to live lifestyles that they might not otherwise have been able to afford. Over the years real estate developers have raised the bar on amenities and lifestyle options that inherently bring people together through a greater sense of community. The ability of community associations to efficiently operate and manage these communities has evolved at a rapid pace, and most homeowners who live in them are well satisfied with the services that they receive. Subsequently, the growth of community associations has been nothing less than phenomenal. It is estimated that the number of associations in the United States will grow from less than 10,000 in the late 1960s to nearly 350,000 by the end of this decade.

Most community associations are legally incorporated nonprofit organizations that operate subject to their governing documents in order to provide community-wide services, regulate activities within the community, and levy and collect assessments that are required to fund association operations. They are grouped into three different categories: homeowners associations, condominiums, and stock housing cooperatives.

A **homeowners association** known as an HOA, that is established by articles of incorporation, manages a community in which homeowners own and maintain their own lots and homes. The HOA owns and maintains the community's commonly owned land, facilities, and amenities. Each homeowner is responsible for the cost of upkeep for his or her own property. They become part of the association's general membership when they take title to that property and, along with the rest of the homeowners, jointly share the expense for the maintenance and upkeep of the portion of the community that is owned by their association.

A **condominium** is a building or complex of buildings containing individually owned apartments. Each apartment is deeded to its owner, who is responsible for its maintenance and upkeep. The apartments are surrounded by the condominium's common elements, such as lobbies, hallways, meeting rooms, elevators, recreation facilities, swimming pools, parking areas, grounds, and the building's structural components. The apartment owners jointly own the building and common elements and are collectively responsible for the cost of their maintenance and upkeep. A condominium association that is created by a declaration of condominium represents the interests of the owners and is responsible for the development's management and operations.

A **stock housing cooperative** is generally a residential apartment building owned and managed by a corporation made up of shareholders who reside in the building. Instead of purchasing an apartment, buyers purchase shares of stock in the corporation. This grants them the right to occupy that apartment for as long as they own their stock. Each shareholder's monthly assessment fees are based upon the number of shares that he or she owns. The assessment payments paid by all the shareholders cover the building's real estate taxes, insurance premiums, building and grounds maintenance, structural repairs, and operating expenses. They are also used to pay principal and interest if there is a mortgage on the property.

These are three different kinds of associations with different legal structures, yet they function in a similar manner with the same core responsibilities: to efficiently manage and operate the association within the framework of a reasonable operating budget and maintain the community's commonly-owned property, protect its architectural integrity, and preserve its property values.

* * * * *

PLANNING LEADERSHIP

Most community associations are well run with established protocols that set forth the manner in which board members, committees, and management staff conduct business, communicate, and carry out responsibilities related to day-to-day operations. Over time, volunteers and staff become used to their daily, weekly, and monthly routines. When change—in the form of a creative planning initiative—is introduced to their routines, they need to be able to turn to their board leaders for consistent, clear direction. Weak leadership direction can lead to confusion and a downward productivity spiral. Missteps and duplications of effort, resulting from a failure to properly coordinate plan activity, tend to damage morale. Volunteers can become territorial about their areas of responsibility leading to close-minded attitudes and negative politics. In the worst cases, this negativity can lead to hard feelings, a loss of motivation to carry out plan initiatives, and a lack of community confidence in the board's agenda. Once planning decisions have been made, it is critical for the board to think and act as one and provide a clear voice that will motivate their volunteer base and the community to support their plan agenda.

> Motivation is the art of getting people to do what you want them to do because they want to do it.
> —Dwight D. Eisenhower,
> 34th president of the United States

The ability to motivate endows leaders with the capacity to influence and inspire their volunteer base to work toward a common goal. Strong and effective board members have clear vision, ideas about what is best for their community, and the things that need be done in order to be successful. Their passion inspires volunteers to share their vision and carry out the association's mission for success. They empower volunteers in order to give them a sense of job ownership and the belief that their work is meaningful.

Once a plan has been initiated, board leaders need to set expectations that do not hold volunteers to unreasonable goals. When reasonable expectations have not been met, they give constructive feedback that does not diminish passion for the job. They also recognize success, make it a point to ensure that volunteers know that their hard work is helping to keep the plan on the right track, and that their efforts are very much appreciated. Exceptional leaders also know that they need to encourage open discussion during the planning process and be consensus builders. They are transparent, share information, and expect to compromise.

Every board member has the ability to lead. They just need to remember that when they are placed in a leadership role, they have to work hard to be effective every day. This is especially important during the planning process when volunteers are working above and beyond their regular comfort area. With good leadership, productivity will prevail, and success is within reach.

* * * * *

ALAN ROBBINS

IS IT TIME TO MOVE AHEAD?

Before making a decision about whether to proceed with planning, board members need to think about the community's condition, the association's current state of affairs, and what the board hopes to achieve. Discussion should be focused on frank questions and honest observations about the board's willingness to support the initiative. Strategic planning requires patience, determination, and a great deal of effort. The benefits of a good plan are well worth the hard work. If a consensus can be reached within the board that it is committed to take on this task, then it's time to move ahead.

CHAPTER II

THE THREE-PHASE PLANNING PROCESS

FOREST GROVE...YOU NEED TO WALK BEFORE YOU RUN

Once the board agreed to move ahead, several of the members were ready to jump right in and schedule a planning session. This was my cue to reinforce the need for patience. I reminded the group that they were dealing with a three-phase planning process and that they were in the early stages of the first phase. Their next steps would be to negotiate a final price for my services and have legal counsel review my contract. They would also need to develop a project timeline. The board would then be in a position to "make things official" by voting to approve the project, timeline, and contract at its next meeting. Once that was done, as facilitator, I could move ahead with preplanning session research, and the board could begin to build consensus about the upcoming initiative within the community and volunteer base. After we reached a clear understanding about first steps and the need to stick to the process at all times, we reviewed basic strategic planning fundamentals and a checklist that outlined the different steps that would need to be carried out in order to complete the entire project. By the time we finished, the board members realized that they would need sixty to ninety days to complete the first phase before they would be ready to conduct the planning session.

ALAN ROBBINS

STRATEGIC PLANNING FUNDAMENTALS

Strategic management involves the development and implementation of major initiatives that are based upon the community's resources and an assessment of the internal and external environment in which the association operates.

Strategic planning is the decision-making process that enables board leadership to define the community and association's direction. It involves an assessment of the strengths, weaknesses, opportunities, and threats that could have a positive or negative impact on the community's well-being and the association's ability to conduct business. These factors enable the board to set priorities, focus energy, allocate resources to pursue clearly defined goals, and develop strategies required to achieve those goals.

Strategic planning nurtures new patterns of thinking within the board and volunteer base, and it encourages support of the collective aspirations of the community. It establishes consensus about desired outcomes and facilitates the ability to monitor progress, assess results, and adjust plan initiatives in order to drive successful outcomes. An effective strategic plan can be likened to a road map. It tells a community association where it is going, how it will get there, and how it will know when it has arrived.

* * * * *

THE CAPSERV STRATEGIC PLANNING PROCESS

Strategic planning is a complex and labor-intensive job. **CAPSERV** simplifies the process by breaking down the project into three manageable phases: (1) Preplanning Session: Preparation and Research, (2) the Planning Session, and (3) Postplanning Session: Plan Implementation.

During the first phase, advance preparation work is done and research is conducted to make certain that planning session participants know what is expected of them, that they understand the expected outcomes of the planning session, and that they have information about the association and community that they will need to develop a viable plan. In the second phase, a planning session is held that is structured to enable participants to stay on task with enough time to thoroughly develop the plan's goals and the strategies required to achieve those goals. During the third and final phase, the strategic plan is written and approved by the board of directors. Association volunteers are then given the opportunity to establish and initiate action steps required to carry out the plan's various strategies, and their work is closely monitored with sufficient board oversight to ensure timely completion of plan initiatives within the framework of the association's budget.

* * * * *

PHASE 1: PREPLANNING SESSION: PREPARATION AND RESEARCH

Once the board of directors has reached a consensus to move ahead and has approved the planning initiative, it needs to identify a capable and qualified planning facilitator.

> Strategic planning is a science…
> Facilitating the planning process
> is an art.

A planning facilitator must have an extensive business management background in order to utilize scientific research principles, analytical methods, mathematical modeling, and statistics to effectively determine the wants and needs of the community's homeowners and review and understand the association's governing documents and financial position.

The facilitator must be able to employ the art of personal communications skills to draw association stakeholders and planning session participants into frank and straightforward discussions and also have the ability to call upon keen observation skills required to ascertain the physical condition of the community.

Actual planning experience is required in order to efficiently organize the planning process, conduct a productive planning session, and write a clear and concise plan. Finding a qualified planning facilitator can be a challenging and daunting task since the board needs to have the confidence to place the plan development initiative in the facilitator's hands. A volunteer that comes from within the association should be able to function in this position without bias related to community or association business matters and possess the business and personal communications skills required to do the job. If an unbiased community volunteer with the right skills and abilities cannot be identified, given the importance of the planning initiative, the board should seek out and employ a trained, professional planning facilitator. Once identified, the facilitator will work closely with the board and association management to set the stage for a successful planning session.

Planning groups sometimes make decisions based on the best information available, only to realize that other information might have been available that could have led to different decisions. A strong planning facilitator works diligently to mitigate this kind of problem. The following checklist outlines the preparation and research steps that the facilitator should take to make sure that the planning group is ready to meet and develop a viable plan.

PLANNING FACILITATOR'S PREPARATION AND RESEARCH CHECKLIST

Part 1: Preparation
- ✓ Review board minutes and the motion to approve the planning initiative and project timeline.
- ✓ Determine if the plan will address general long-term planning issues or specific matters of board concern.
- ✓ Identify planning session participants.
- ✓ Confirm the planning session date, time, and location.

MASTER PLAN

- ✓ Communicate with the management staff. Provide written instructions to (1) reserve the meeting room, (2) set the room up for the meeting, (3) make arrangements to provide meal service, and (4) provide meeting supplies.
- ✓ One month prior to the planning session, e-mail an invitation to participate to all planning session participants. Advise participants if a meal or refreshments are being provided. The invitation should reinforce expectations related to the purpose and proposed outcomes of the session. Include an RSVP to request that participants confirm if they plan to attend and participate.
- ✓ Two weeks prior to the planning session, send a reminder e-mail to planning session participants. Request that invited participants who have not responded to the invitation advise management if they plan to attend.
- ✓ One week prior to the meeting, communicate with management to confirm that they are prepared for the meeting in accordance with their original instructions.

Part 2: Research
- ✓ Review state association governance laws, the association's governing documents, policy resolutions, administrative resolutions, and pertinent operating procedures to determine how they might impact planning goals, strategies, and action steps.
- ✓ Review the association's latest financial statements, budget, audit, and reserve study or update. Look for financial red flags that warrant discussion during the planning session. If red flags are noted, discuss them with the board president and general manager to determine if they can be discussed at the planning session.
- ✓ Review the association's covenants guidelines and latest covenants inspection and enforcement status reports.

- ✓ Have the association conduct a community-wide survey. Review and analyze the survey responses. Send the results and analysis to the planning session participants for review prior to the session.
- ✓ Interview board officers, committee chairs, and management staff. Determine if any of these key stakeholders have specific concerns about the community, association operations, or the association's finances.
- ✓ Conduct a general inspection of the property. Assess the condition of the community's physical infrastructure, grounds maintenance, and general appearance. Observe the overall streetscape in order to form a general opinion about homeowner compliance with association covenants and property-maintenances rules.

* * * * *

PHASE 2: THE PLANNING SESSION: PLAN DEVELOPMENT

Room setup should help to facilitate discussion. Participants should be seated at tables so that they can comfortably take notes and use reference material that may be provided. Name cards should be placed in front of participants so that the facilitator can address them by name. Audience style seating should be available off to the side or behind the participants to accommodate meeting visitors. The facilitator will work with an erasable whiteboard, easels, and large "sticky sheet" notepads. As discussions take place, the facilitator makes notes on the whiteboard. At the end of each discussion final notes are transferred to a sticky sheet and placed on the wall for reference purposes throughout the day. Those sheets will also be used for reference purposes, after the planning session, when the first draft of the plan is written. The planning session should be recorded, as a safeguard, to ensure that there is a complete record of everything that was discussed at the meeting.

MASTER PLAN

The keys to an interesting and productive planning session are organization, reasonable discipline, and the promotion of an atmosphere that empowers all the participants to get their ideas on the table. Everyone should be drawn into the discussion without letting anyone overpower the group. The facilitator must know how to keep the discussion on topic, when to stay on a particular subject, and when it is time to move on. All opinions should be considered, and the tone of the discussion should be civil. A good facilitator must be able to observe the entire group and read body language and facial expressions to make sure that less vocal participants, who tend to fade into the background, are not overlooked.

Community volunteers are sometimes inclined to want to spend as little time in meetings as possible; therefore, board members, committee chairs, and committee members should know up front about the amount of time that they will need to commit for the planning session. The **CAPSERV** process generally calls for one full-day, eight-hour session running from ten in the morning to five in the afternoon with an option to extend the session for one hour. If there is a concern that planning may not be completed in one day, two slightly shorter back-to-back sessions that allow for more discussion time are an option. Sessions can become tedious and tiring. The session workday should be broken down into one-hour discussions with five-minute breaks between discussions. A light working lunch should be provided during the session, and refreshments should be on hand throughout the day. While discipline regarding discussion is important, the atmosphere should be casual. Participants should be free to take restroom breaks when needed. Cellular phones should be turned off or on "vibrate" mode. If someone needs to take a call, they should have their discussion outside of the meeting room. Absolutely no texting should take place in the room since it tends to distract the group.

At the beginning of the planning session, the facilitator welcomes the group, makes introductions, and reviews the session's purpose and objectives. This is followed by a quick review of the "rules of engagement" for the meeting. Robert's Rules of Order do not apply. The facilitator is in charge with the responsibility to make sure that the group stays on task and that discussion flows in a productive manner. In most states, community associations are required to hold general meetings in a public forum. This means that homeowners are allowed to attend; however, only planning session participants are allowed to speak during planning discussion.

Upon completion of the facilitator's opening comments, the facilitator and session participants move into planning mode, at which time they put together a strategic plan that will ultimately include the following:

- The community's vision statement and the association's mission statement
- An analysis of the community and association's most significant strengths, weaknesses, opportunities, and threats
- Goals to achieve the plan's mission and strategies to reach those goals
- Communications and feedback mechanisms that will facilitate the distribution of planning activity status updates to homeowners and volunteers and their subsequent feedback that will enable the board of directors to manage plan activity
- Board monitoring and plan project management procedures

(Note: During the third and final phase of the planning process, after the plan has been written and approved by the board of directors, designated association volunteers will have the opportunity to establish and implement action steps required to carry out the plan's strategies.)

* * * * *

MASTER PLAN

PHASE 3: POSTPLANNING SESSION: PLAN IMPLEMENTATION

Writing and Approving the Plan

The facilitator's first order of business in the third phase of the planning process is to write a plan draft. The draft should be completed and distributed within one week after the session in order to give participants the opportunity to review the document while the discussion that took place during planning is still relatively fresh in their minds. While writing style and grammar are important, the real focus should be on accurately reflecting the group's final decisions about each of the plan's components. The purpose of the review is to comment about material matters rather than to edit the document. Suggestions for changes should relate to matters of substance in the draft that do not agree with decisions that were made during the session. Upon receipt of the planning group's comments and suggestions for content changes, the facilitator revises the draft and sends it to the board of directors for final approval. Once the plan has been approved, the association's volunteers can move ahead with action step development and implementation.

Project Management and Board Oversight

The board of directors needs to take great care to see to it that the planning process does not falter after the planning session. It happens in the best of associations. Strategic plans are developed amid a flurry of activity. Then the volunteers return to their regular day jobs, and real life sets in as the association begins to focus on its day-to-day operations. Pressing issues crowd out strategic thought and divert board member and committee volunteer attention. After a while, volunteers begin to lose sight of the plan's goals and strategies. This leads to a failure to execute. This can be avoided with strong project management and timely, effective board oversight.

Planning project execution begins when the board of directors tasks volunteers with the responsibility to develop and implement action steps that will be required to carry out the plan's various strategies. As each action step is developed and implemented, a description of the work that will be done is entered in the plan along with the name of the committee or volunteer responsible for doing the job and its target completion date. The plan is then updated on a quarterly basis to provide current project status. To facilitate oversight, volunteers present monthly activity reports at board meetings that enable the board to closely monitor progress, address priorities, and ensure that work is proceeding within the framework of the association's budget.

* * * * *

GAUGING YOUR ASSOCIATION'S SUCCESS

The strategic plan's initiatives have been carried out and all planning work has been completed. The board has provided the leadership needed to accomplish the association's mission, and volunteers have worked hard to fulfill the community's vision for the future. Does this mean that the plan has been a success?

To determine if the association has been successful, the board can begin by reviewing the association's core responsibilities: to efficiently manage and operate the association within the framework of a reasonable budget, maintain the community's common property, protect its architectural integrity, and preserve its property values. Once these responsibilities have been reviewed, the board members need to answer the following questions:

- Are the community's streetscapes, common area landscaping, and open green space well-kept and attractive?
- Have the community's amenities, including swimming pools, athletic areas, playgrounds, and parking lots, been properly maintained?

- As the clubhouse and common buildings aged, have they been refurbished in order to keep up with the times?
- If the board is responsible for a homeowners association, have the association's covenants rules, architectural guidelines, and maintenance requirements for privately owned homes and lots been successfully enforced?
- If the board is dealing with a condominium or housing cooperative, are the buildings well cared for and in good condition? Have the lobby, hallways, and common rooms been redecorated to give them a fresh, new look?
- Has the association been operating within the framework of a well-balanced budget, and have sufficient repair and replacement reserve funds been accumulated to ensure that the community's infrastructure will not be neglected due to a lack of funds?
- Has the association operated smoothly with a productive, conflict-free work environment for board members and committees?
- Have homeowners been satisfied with the services provided by the association?
- Are community property values keeping pace with property values in similar communities in the general area?

To answer these questions, the board should begin by touring the community and view it through an objective lens in order to determine if its appearance meets the expectations that were set forth in the plan. It should reaffirm that the association carried out its objectives within the plan's financial guidelines and confirm that it continues to operate within budget. It should look closely at property value trends in the general area to determine if values in the community have kept pace with the local real estate market. Before forming a final conclusion, the board should conduct a follow up survey to determine if homeowners are satisfied with the association's progress and the condition of the community.

If the answers to the board's questions are yes and feedback from the community is positive, the planning effort has met with success. If any of the answers are no, or if there are negative trends in the survey, the board should review the plan, determine what went wrong, and take action to rectify the deficiencies until it is satisfied that they have been corrected.

* * * * *

LINKING THE BUDGET TO THE PLAN

Some associations attempt to tie their strategic plans to their current operating budget that was developed prior to planning. This tends to be a serious mistake since the budget could not possibly take into account the plan's future funding needs, resulting in a restriction of capital and limitation of project initiatives. In order for a strategic plan to fully address the association and community's needs, it must have 100% funding capacity.

The key to attaining full-funding capacity is to develop the plan early enough in a given year so that all the plan's project proposals and associated expenses are completed in time to be included in the association's upcoming year's annual budget process. This will ensure that the new budget provides for potential increases in operating expenses, funds will be set aside to pay for capital expenditures, and reserve contributions will be adjusted to cover modifications to the community's repair and replacement reserves.

CHAPTER III

EFFECTIVE COMMUNICATION AND SURVEYS

FOREST GROVE...THE COST OF POOR COMMUNICATIONS

It's unfortunate but true... Apathy reigns supreme! Homeowners do not make it a point to attend regular board meetings unless they have personal issues that need to be addressed, and tend to leave the meetings once they have finished discussing their problems. They don't bother to read newsletters and communications, and most won't serve as volunteers. This is understandable since, in today's hectic world, most homeowners rarely have the time or interest to get involved with their association.

Nonetheless, astute board members recognize that when important decisions need to be made about major initiatives, community input should be part of their decision-making process. Board members need to utilize every method at their disposal to reach out to the community in order to get homeowners' attention and feedback before they move ahead with their plans.

No one ever wants to believe that they are poor communicators, but Forest Grove's board had to admit that during past attempts to carry out long-range planning projects, it "dropped the communications ball." Like most associations, homeowner turnout at their meetings was nominal. In order to get the pulse of the community, board members could only rely on input from a few committee volunteers and talks with their neighbors. Surveys had never been done to determine what the majority of homeowners might want or need. Opportunities to solicit input at town hall meetings or by e-mail blasts were missed. The board clearly did not have an understanding about satisfaction levels related to the quality of association services or the community's appearance. As plans were developed and implemented, no real effort was made to build homeowner and volunteer consensus or manage expectations about plan initiatives. It didn't take long for the directors to get my message and realize that their failure to communicate came at a cost...strategic plans that did not give the community what it wanted, months of wasted time and effort implementing plans that were destined to fail, and a volunteer base that was burned out and rapidly losing motivation.

THE NEED FOR PROACTIVE COMMUNICATION

A homeowner who has been elected to the board of directors has been entrusted with the authority to make decisions that can maintain the current state of affairs or drive change that could have a positive or negative impact on their community's future. Decisions that could lead to significant change should never be made in a vacuum that is devoid of outside input. Every homeowner has the right to expect the board of directors to be a conduit that disseminates information about important issues and encourages feedback that can be part of its decision-making process. In order to be drivers of positive change, the board must master proactive communications.

Proactive communication is a term associated with the process of communicating and exchanging ideas, information, and news as a relationship-building strategy. Its use can benefit the board and association in a number of ways:

- By routinely reaching out to provide information and requesting feedback, the board is in a better position to anticipate homeowner wants and needs.

- Homeowner confidence in the association increases when the board regularly provides information about pending projects.
- By making an effort to transparently provide information and solicit feedback, it shows that the board cares about homeowner opinions, helping to build a foundation for community engagement and trust.
- Ongoing dialogue between the board and homeowners reduces the possibility of unwanted surprises that can lead to conflict between the association and the community.

* * * * *

CONSENSUS BUILDING AND MANAGING EXPECTATIONS

When embarking on a strategic planning initiative, proactive communication helps to build consensus and manage expectations amongst the board, volunteer base, and community.

The first link in creating a strong consensus chain is to ensure that there are no misunderstandings within the board about what will be done. Written procedures, a project timeline, and a motion to approve the planning project should be sent to the board for review prior to voting on the measure. Once the official vote has taken place, and the motion has been approved, all board members should make a concerted effort to support the effort, ensure that clear and concise directions are given to volunteers at all times, and collectively approve and stand behind all communications about the project that are sent to the community.

The next link in the consensus building chain involves bidirectional communications between the board and committees to ensure that volunteers have a positive sense of project ownership. It should begin when the board is formulating the steps that will be taken to develop and carry out the plan and continue throughout the planning process. Committee chairs and members should be encouraged to be present during board discussions so that they can gain an understanding about the reasons for doing the plan and the project's expected outcomes. This will also give them the opportunity to provide feedback about project rollout, plan implementation, and their role in contributing to its success.

The final link in the chain is for the board to build and maintain community consensus by keeping homeowners in the communications loop at all times. Progress updates should be positive and creative, but they should also be carefully crafted in order to manage expectations and reduce the possibility of unnecessary disappointment about work results. Homeowners need to believe that they also have a stake in the planning initiative. It is important to let them know that their input will be a critical part of the board's decision-making process and that they will have the opportunity to provide feedback through surveys, board of directors meetings, and town hall meetings.

* * * * *

EFFECTIVE SURVEYS

Surveys are powerful information collection tools that a community association can use to determine the opinions of its general membership. No other means of communication can provide this kind of broad capability to gather data that, when properly organized, interpreted, and analyzed, can be used to draw conclusions and make decisions that will have a profound impact on the community and the manner in which the association conducts business.

Homeowners are not inclined to complete long and complicated surveys. **CAPSERV** planning surveys are designed to mitigate "survey fatigue." Participants are asked to answer a short series of multiple-choice questions and to complete four simple response lists. Their responses provide a broad range of data, yet the survey is short enough to be completed within a reasonable amount of time.

Multiple-choice questions are easy to answer since they simply require respondents to select one option from a list of predetermined answers. The following example illustrates how this works:

MASTER PLAN

- **Question: "How satisfied are you with our community association's services?"**
- **Response Options:**
  o Very satisfied.
  o Satisfied.
  o Neutral—I am neither satisfied nor dissatisfied.
  o Dissatisfied.
  o Very dissatisfied.
- **Analysis: Based upon the answers to this question, a survey analyst can easily determine the percentage of satisfied participants versus the percentage that were dissatisfied.**

Assuming that two hundred respondents answered this question...

  o 147 respondents (73.5% of the response pool) indicated that they were satisfied or very satisfied;
  o 21 respondents (10.5% of the response pool) were neither satisfied nor dissatisfied;
  o 32 respondents (16.0% of the response pool) indicated that they were dissatisfied or very dissatisfied; and
  o the response ratio of 73.5% to 16.0% indicates that a majority of households in the community were satisfied with association services, with a caveat that the association should aspire to increase homeowner satisfaction.

Response lists enable survey participants to provide narrative feedback about the community and association that is not limited to stock yes/no or multiple-choice responses. This promotes in-depth statements in each participant's own words, giving insight into their perspectives about the subject in question. **CAPSERV** surveys usually contain the following lists:

1. List up to five association or community strengths that could be enhanced.

2. List up to five association or community weaknesses that need to be addressed or corrected.
3. List up to five opportunities that could have a positive impact on our community or our association's ability to conduct business.
4. List up to five threats that could have a negative impact on our community or our association's ability to conduct business.

* * * * *

DATA REVIEW

A statistician engages in the science of collecting and analyzing numerical data. It can take years of college study for an individual with an aptitude for math and science to learn statistical analysis, followed by years of practical application, before he or she can gain enough experience to be considered an authority in their field.

Frankly, it does not take a statistician to develop a simple survey that is meant to gather the opinions of a community's homeowners or to quantify and analyze the survey's results. The whole purpose of the design and structure of a **CAPSERV** planning survey is to simplify the process. It is easy to work with since analysts only have to deal with two types of feedback.

The multiple-choice questions in the survey are quantifiable since they are measured numerically. There are five possible answer options for each question. Only one can be chosen. If an online survey tool is used to conduct the survey, data analysis does not take a great deal of effort. The survey tool will organize and group the answers for each question by option choice. It will then calculate the number and percentage of respondents that picked each option, providing insight into homeowner opinions about the issue. Survey analysts are not required to crunch numbers. They simply have to review the results of the electronic calculations.

Response lists are qualitative in nature calling for careful review and interpretation. Feedback in these lists tends to be subjective and nuanced. Some of that feedback may not be relevant. Nonetheless, these lists will still yield a good deal of significant information. Each survey participant's meaningful statements are cross-catalogued against similar comments that were made by other respondents in order to identify patterns, themes, and trends. Given the volume of narrative responses that could be received, this process can be time-consuming, but analysis does not require complex mathematics. It merely requires a lot of reading and a bit of common sense. In the end, the effort is worthwhile since survey participants provide feedback in their own words that can be used to uncover issues that might have otherwise been overlooked.

A review of the patterns, themes, and trends identified in the survey's response lists, combined with the answers to the survey's multiple-choice questions, enables the board and planning group to determine the association and community's overall strengths, weaknesses, opportunities, and threats (SWOT). A **SWOT Analysis** is then conducted during the planning session to organize the most significant of these factors into a short, manageable list that is presented in a two-by-two easy-to-read grid. This information is used to drive planning discussion and develop plan goals and strategies.

SWOT ANALYSIS	
Strengths, Weaknesses, Opportunities, and Threats	
STRENGTHS	**OPPORTUNITIES**
• **Strength** • **Strength** • **Strength** • **Strength**	• **Opportunity** • **Opportunity** • **Opportunity** • **Opportunity**

WEAKNESSES	THREATS
• Weakness • Weakness • Weakness • Weakness	• Threat • Threat • Threat • Threat

* * * * *

SURVEY PROCESS MANAGEMENT

The target response rate for a community association survey that is easy to complete and return to the association tends to range from 20% to 30% of the households in the community. This range provides a reasonable representation of homeowner opinions. Failure to conduct a survey in an organized and efficient manner could result in an insufficient number of responses that is well below that range, undermining the statistical validity of the data collected. If an association cannot trust its survey results, the effort made to obtain the information will have been a waste of time. The following process management steps can be followed in order to maximize the probability of survey success.

Survey Process Management Checklist

- ✓ Create a timeline from project inception through completion.
- ✓ Develop written project procedures.
- ✓ Develop multiple-choice questions and open-ended response lists.
- ✓ Determine the survey mode…electronic or paper.
- ✓ If the mode is electronic, select a service provider that offers an on-line survey tool that suits the association's needs.

MASTER PLAN

- ✓ Develop an inviting and simple-to-use survey.
- ✓ Confirm the target respondent pool... All households in the community, one contact per household.
- ✓ Have the survey procedures, timeline, service provider, and survey draft approved by the board of directors.
- ✓ Prepare to launch... Send a preliminary notification to the general membership about the pending survey.
- ✓ Launch... Distribute the survey. Set a thirty-day response deadline.
- ✓ Follow up with all households at the end of each week during the response period to reinforce the need to complete the survey and increase homeowner participation.
- ✓ Gather and track responses as they are received.
- ✓ After reaching the survey response deadline, distribute the results to the board of directors, planning group, and the association's general membership. Distribution should be completed early enough to give the board and planning group sufficient time to review the results prior to the planning session.
- ✓ Utilize the survey data to draw conclusions that will drive planning discussion about plan goals and strategies.

CHAPTER IV

THE CAPSERV SIX-POINT STRATEGIC PLAN MODEL

FOREST GROVE...A WELL-WRITTEN PLAN

When we finished the planning session, everyone was elated about how well things went. The group followed process, had a good planning session, and came up with a number of great ideas, yet I could see that some of members of the group were anxious about something. It didn't take much prompting for them to voice their concerns. Sure...they had the makings of a good plan, but there was so much information to digest. How were they going to get it all down on paper and come to an agreement about its written contents? This led to a short but spirited debate. It was obvious that they weren't coming to a consensus about how to proceed. It was time for me to step in and clear the air.

I told them that writing the plan was a straightforward task and reminded them about the key components of the **CAPSERV** strategic planning model. It was all about organization. The model was a template. It was my responsibility to write the plan. I simply had to accurately transfer their decisions to that template. Our planning session was on a Friday. I indicated that I would complete a written draft and send it to the group for review and comment toward the middle of the following week.

MASTER PLAN

I set some ground rules to make certain that the review process ran smoothly. The decisions about the plan's goals and strategies that were made during the planning session were well articulated and precise. They were good decisions. Review was not supposed to be an opportunity for anyone to second-guess the group's intent. I made it clear that its purpose was to ensure that their decisions were accurately captured in the written document. Feedback about the draft should only cover changes that would be needed to correct material misstatements. Upon receipt of everyone's comments, I would complete a final draft that could be submitted to the board of directors for discussion and approval at their next monthly meeting. Any further revisions could only be made at the sole discretion of the board. Once approval was received, the association's volunteers could then develop the actions steps required to carry out the plan's strategies and achieve its long-range goals.

The planning group was comfortable with the next steps. It was time to write the plan.

THE MODEL

A well-written strategic plan is a document that provides comprehensive information about all elements and aspects of the plan in an objective, concise, clear, and easy-to-understand manner. The **CAPSERV** Six-Point Strategic Plan Model serves as a template that facilitates an organized logical flow of the ideas expressed during planning discussion and accurately sets forth the planning group's specific decisions about the plan's goals and strategies. Its core components are the following:

1. The Community Vision Statement
2. The Association's Mission Statement
3. Strengths, Weaknesses, Opportunities, and Threats
4. Goals, Strategies, and Action Steps
5. Communications and Feedback
6. Plan Review and Modification

THE COMMUNITY VISION STATEMENT defines what a community aspires to be. It is a statement about what is most important to its homeowners and focuses on their shared values. It sets standards of excellence, inspires enthusiasm and commitment, and is likely to lead to a better future. A good vision statement has the following characteristics:

- It is short enough to be easy to communicate yet broad enough to cover a variety of perspectives.
- It is clear enough to be understood by the community and the association's volunteers.

THE ASSOCIATION'S MISSION STATEMENT defines a community association's reason for existing. It expresses the association's purpose, describes what it will do in order to achieve the community's vision, and creates a sense of identity for the association's volunteers. It is the driving force behind everything that the association does to benefit the community.

STRENGTHS, WEAKNESSES, OPPORTUNITIES, AND THREATS are primary drivers for consideration when developing the plan's goals and strategies.

- **Strengths** are positive characteristics that could be addressed to enhance the association and community.
- **Weaknesses** are negative characteristics that need to be addressed to resolve association and community deficiencies.
- **Opportunities** are current or potential circumstances that could have a positive impact on the community or the association's ability to conduct business.
- **Threats** are current or potential circumstances that could have a negative impact on the community or impede the association's ability to conduct business.

MASTER PLAN

GOALS, STRATEGIES, AND ACTION STEPS outline what the association's volunteers must do to successfully bring about the plan's desired outcomes.

- **Goals** are broad objectives that must be reached in order to accomplish the association's mission. These objectives generally have quantifiable or qualitatively measured results.
- **Strategies** are plans of action designed to achieve each goal.
- **Action steps** refer to specific tasks that will be executed to carry out each strategy. The plan identifies who is responsible for each task, its target completion date, and current work status.

The **COMMUNICATIONS AND FEEDBACK** component establishes procedures for the periodic distribution of project status updates to the community and subsequent feedback from homeowners that can be used by board members when they make planning decisions.

The **PLAN REVIEW AND MODIFICATION** component establishes the oversight process that enables the board to efficiently review, direct, and manage the work that is being done to carry out plan initiatives.

ADDENDUM A

THE 2011 FOREST GROVE COMMUNITY SURVEY

2011 FOREST GROVE COMMUNITY SURVEY
Introduction

The Forest Grove Board of Directors is in the process of developing a long-term strategic plan. We invite you to participate in a survey that will enable you to provide feedback that will help us to make decisions that will shape our community's future.

In the first part of this survey, we ask you to answer eleven multiple-choice questions about basic association services and the condition of our community. In the second part, we request that you complete four short response lists. These lists will give you the opportunity to tell us, in your own words, about important issues that our association may need to deal with now or in the future.

Survey responses are limited to one per household. We ask that you respond no later than April 15. Once all the responses have been collected, the results of the survey will be distributed for homeowner review.

Your feedback will be a very import part of our decision-making process. We look forward to hearing from you.

Please continue on the following page to begin part 1 of this survey.

2011 FOREST GROVE COMMUNITY SURVEY
Part 1: General Questions

1. **How satisfied are you with our community association's services?**
   o Very satisfied.
   o Satisfied.
   o I am neither satisfied nor unsatisfied.
   o Unsatisfied.
   o Very unsatisfied.

2. **I get a sufficient amount of information about association business from our board of directors.**
   o I strongly agree.
   o I agree.
   o I neither agree nor disagree.
   o I disagree.
   o I strongly disagree.

3. **How satisfied are you with the level of service that you receive from the management company?**
   o Very satisfied.
   o Satisfied.
   o I am neither satisfied nor unsatisfied.
   o Unsatisfied.
   o Very unsatisfied.

4. **Forest Grove Community Association gives me good value for my monthly assessment payments.**
   o I strongly agree.
   o I agree.
   o I neither agree nor disagree.
   o I disagree.
   o I strongly disagree

2011 FOREST GROVE COMMUNITY SURVEY
Part 1: General Questions

5. **I am familiar with our architectural covenants rules.**
   o   I strongly agree.
   o   I agree.
   o   I neither agree nor disagree.
   o   I disagree.
   o   I strongly disagree.

6. **Our architectural covenants rules are reasonable.**
   o   I strongly agree.
   o   I agree.
   o   I neither agree nor disagree.
   o   I disagree.
   o   I strongly disagree.

7. **How satisfied are you with the appearance of the landscaping in our community's common areas?**
   o   Very satisfied.
   o   Satisfied.
   o   I am neither satisfied nor unsatisfied.
   o   Unsatisfied.
   o   Very unsatisfied.

8. **How satisfied are you with the interior decorating and furnishings in our clubhouse?**
   o   Very satisfied.
   o   Satisfied.
   o   I am neither satisfied nor unsatisfied.
   o   Unsatisfied.
   o   Very unsatisfied.

2011 FOREST GROVE COMMUNITY SURVEY
Part 1: General Questions

9. Our association website provides useful news and information about our community.
    - o I strongly agree.
    - o I agree.
    - o I neither agree nor disagree.
    - o I disagree.
    - o I strongly disagree.

10. I regularly read e-mails from our community association and board of directors.
    - o I strongly agree.
    - o I agree.
    - o I neither agree nor disagree.
    - o I disagree.
    - o I strongly disagree.

11. I am interested in volunteering to join an association committee.
    - o I strongly agree.
    - o I agree.
    - o I neither agree nor disagree.
    - o I disagree.
    - o I strongly disagree.

Please continue on the following page to complete the response lists in part 2 of this survey.

2011 FOREST GROVE COMMUNITY SURVEY
Part 2: Response Lists

List up to five association or community strengths that could be enhanced. (Maximum 20 words per comment.)

Strength 1: _____

Strength 2: _____

Strength 3: _____

Strength 4: _____

Strength 5: _____

List up to five association or community weaknesses that need to be addressed and corrected. (Maximum 20 words per comment.)

Weakness 1: _____

Weakness 2: _____

Weakness 3: _____

Weakness 4: _____

Weakness 5: _____

MASTER PLAN

2011 FOREST GROVE COMMUNITY SURVEY
Part 2: Response Lists

List up to five opportunities that could have a positive impact on our community or our association's ability to conduct business. (Maximum 20 words per comment.)

Opportunity 1: _____

Opportunity 2: _____

Opportunity 3: _____

Opportunity 4: _____

Opportunity 5: _____

List up to five threats that could have a negative impact on our community or impede our association's ability to conduct business. (Maximum 20 words per comment.)

Threat 1: _____

Threat 2: _____

Threat 3: _____

Threat 4: _____

Threat 5: _____

2011 FOREST GROVE COMMUNITY SURVEY
Survey Submission

Thank you for participating.
Click on the icon to submit your survey.

Submit

ADDENDUM B

THE 2011 SURVEY RESULTS AND SWOT ANALYSIS

2011 SURVEY RESULTS

The board of directors determined that the response rate for this survey should fall within a range of 20% to 30% of the households in the community in order for the data that was collected to be sufficient for planning purposes. The association received 227 responses (36% of the 624 households in Forest Grove). This was over the target range and well above the survey's minimum threshold requirement, resulting in a high level of confidence that the data collected represents the general opinions of the community.

Multiple-Choice Questions

Answers provided by survey participants were grouped by option choice. The percentage of respondents that chose each option was then calculated. Highlighted percentages reflect the opinions of the majority of the homeowners that answered each question.

1. **How satisfied are you with our community association services?**
   - **5% responded: Very satisfied.**
   - **70% responded: Satisfied.**
   - 14% responded: I am neither satisfied nor unsatisfied.
   - 5% responded: Unsatisfied.
   - 3% responded: Very unsatisfied.
   - 3% did not respond to this question.

2. **I get a sufficient amount of information about association business from our board of directors.**
   - 1% responded: I strongly agree.
   - 15% responded: I agree.
   - 12% responded: I neither agree nor disagree.
   - **53% responded: I disagree.**
   - **17% responded: I strongly disagree**
   - 2% did not respond to this question.

MASTER PLAN

3. **How satisfied are you with the level of service that you receive from the management company?**
   - **11% responded: Very satisfied.**
   - **72% responded: Satisfied.**
   - 9% responded: I am neither satisfied nor unsatisfied.
   - 4% responded: Unsatisfied.
   - 2% responded: Very unsatisfied.
   - 2% did not respond to this question.

4. **Forest Grove Community Association gives me good value for my monthly assessment payments.**
   - 4% responded: I strongly agree.
   - 22% responded: I agree.
   - 17% responded: I neither agree nor disagree.
   - **42% responded: I disagree.**
   - **11% responded: I strongly disagree**
   - 4% did not respond to this question.

5. **I am familiar with our architectural covenants rules.**
   - 3% responded: I strongly agree.
   - 14% responded: I agree.
   - **28% responded: I neither agree nor disagree.**
   - **42% responded: I disagree.**
   - **7% responded: I strongly disagree.**
   - 6% did not respond to this question.

6. **Our architectural covenants rules are reasonable.**
   - **12% responded: I strongly agree.**
   - **24% responded: I agree.**
   - **36% responded: I neither agree nor disagree.**
   - 11% responded: I disagree.
   - 9% responded: I strongly disagree.
   - 8% did not respond to this question.

7. **How satisfied are you with the appearance of the landscaping in our community's common areas?**
   - 3% responded: Very satisfied
   - 31% Responded: Satisfied
   - 22% responded: I am neither satisfied nor unsatisfied.
   - **34% responded: Unsatisfied.**
   - **8% responded: Very unsatisfied.**
   - 2% did not respond to this question.

8. **How satisfied are you with the interior decorating and furnishings in our clubhouse?**
   - 1% responded: Very satisfied.
   - 19% responded: Satisfied.
   - 12% responded: I am neither satisfied nor unsatisfied.
   - **38% responded: Unsatisfied.**
   - **27% responded: Very unsatisfied.**
   - 3% did not respond to this question.

9. **Our association website provides useful news and information about our community.**
   - 6% responded: I strongly agree.
   - 26% responded: I agree.
   - **26% responded: I neither agree nor disagree.**
   - **32% responded: I disagree.**
   - **7% responded: I strongly disagree.**
   - 3% did not respond to this question.

10. **I regularly read e-mails from our community association and board of directors.**
    - 11% responded: I strongly agree.
    - 22% responded: I agree.
    - **18% responded: I neither agree nor disagree.**
    - **32% responded: I disagree.**
    - **13% responded: I strongly disagree.**
    - 4% did not respond to this question.

MASTER PLAN

11. I am interested in volunteering to join an association committee.
- 6% responded: I strongly agree.
- 18% responded: I agree.
- 12% responded: I neither agree nor disagree.
- **42% responded: I disagree.**
- **17% responded: I strongly disagree.**
- 5% did not respond to this question.

Response List Feedback

More than 800 individual comments were provided in the survey's 4 response lists. Response trends and patterns reflect homeowner opinions that, when combined with the answers to the survey's multiple-choice questions, help to develop an understanding about issues that warrant planning consideration.

List 1: Strengths
- Beautiful wooded neighborhood.
- Large lots and attractive stately homes.
- The original design concept for the community capitalizes on the area's natural wooded appearance.
- The community has miles of paved walkways in its wooded areas.
- Forest Grove is a relatively private neighborhood.
- The central location of the clubhouse and recreation facilities encourages their use as a central gathering place for the community's residents.
- The layout of roadways in the community facilitates smooth traffic flow.
- The association does business with a strong management company.
- Basic association operations run smoothly.
- The management company's seasoned staff is responsive and has a good working relationship with our homeowners.

- Assessment payment delinquency is low, and the association's financial condition is healthy.
- The landscaping company does an adequate job maintaining the association's open green spaces and landscaping.

List 2: Weaknesses
- The board of directors does not do enough to inform homeowners about the association.
- Most homeowners in the community are apathetic about association activities.
- The number of volunteers is insufficient.
- Board leadership is not engaging or motivating the association's volunteer base.
- The board has missed opportunities to recruit homeowners who are willing to serve as association volunteers.
- The association's website is underutilized.
- The association's e-mail blast program is weak.
- There are too many covenant violations in the community, including a lack of home maintenance, failure to mow lawns, failure to maintain landscape beds, and changes in trim colors from natural earth tone colors to bright primary and pastel colors.
- The association's covenants inspection program is weak.
- The asphalt walking paths in the wooded areas of the community are in extremely poor and unsafe condition.
- Landscaping beds in the community's common areas need to be refreshed and updated.
- The appearance of the main entrance to the community is weak and unimpressive.
- The landscaping around the clubhouse needs to be replaced.
- The clubhouse parking lot needs major repairs.
- The interior decorations and furnishings in the clubhouse are out dated and in poor condition.

MASTER PLAN

- Workout equipment in the clubhouse needs to be replaced.
- The association website is weak and underutilized.
- Many homeowners do not pay attention to association e-mail blasts.

List 3: Opportunities
- A number of homeowners have indicated that they would be willing to volunteer for association committees.
- Lower interest rates may help to increase community home values.
- Pending state legislation may support stronger community association assessment collection rights.

List 4: Threats
- The nationwide financial crisis may result in increased association assessment payment delinquency.
- The association does not have a full understanding about pending state legislation that may have a negative impact on community associations.
- Increasing competition from new housing developments in the area may have a negative impact on Forest Grove home values.
- The development of a new four-lane road on the western border of the community may have a negative impact on homes adjacent to the proposed roadway.
- The development of strip shopping centers in the immediate area could have a negative impact on traffic around our community.
- Redistricting of schools' boundaries could have a negative impact on families with children in our community.

The SWOT Analysis on the following pages identify Forest Grove's most significant strengths, weaknesses, opportunities, and threats.

2011 FOREST GROVE SWOT ANALYSIS	
STRENGTHS	OPPORTUNITIES
<ul><li>Wooded neighborhood with large lots and stately homes.</li><li>Miles of paved walking paths.</li><li>Relatively private neighborhood.</li><li>Central clubhouse and recreation facilities.</li><li>Strong management company and responsive staff.</li><li>Smooth-running association operations.</li><li>Low-assessment payment delinquency and healthy association financial condition.</li><li>Landscaping company does an adequate job.</li></ul>	<ul><li>A number of homeowners are interested in volunteering to serve as committee members.</li><li>Pending state legislation may support stronger assessment collection rights.</li></ul>

MASTER PLAN

WEAKNESSES	THREATS
• Board does not keep community informed about association activities. • Weak association website. • Volunteers are not motivated. • Not enough volunteers. • Board and committee members need training. Association operating polices need to be reinforced. • Weak covenants program. Too many covenant violations. • Asphalt clubhouse parking lot and walking paths are in poor condition. • Common area landscape beds are weak and need to be replaced. • Weak signage. Main entrance to community, clubhouse, and villages are unimpressive. • Shabby clubhouse interior and outdated exercise equipment.	• Nationwide financial crisis may increase assessment payment delinquency and lower community home values. • Increasing competition from new housing developments in the area may have a negative impact on Forest Grove home values. • Development of new strip centers in the area could have a negative impact on traffic around our community. • Redistricting of school boundaries may have a negative impact on families with children in our community.

ADDENDUM C

THE 2011 FOREST GROVE STRATEGIC PLAN

A note about the plan...

The board of directors approved Forest Grove's strategic plan on June 16, 2011. At that time, the plan contained its long-term goals and strategies with the understanding that actions steps required to carry out those strategies would be developed and added at a later date. That work was completed and the action steps were added to the plan during the following ninety days.

This version of the plan, dated September 30, 2011, provided information about each action step's project status, including details about the work to be done, the committee or volunteer responsible for carrying out the task, and its target completion date. During the plan's three-year duration period, it was updated at the end of each quarter to report changes in project status until all work was completed in 2014.

MASTER PLAN

2011 FOREST GROVE COMMUNITY ASSOCIATION STRATEGIC PLAN LATEST QUARTERLY UPDATE – SEPTEMBER 30, 2011

INTRODUCTION

The 2011 Forest Grove Community Association Strategic Plan, approved by the board of directors on July 16, 2011, addresses long-term issues that have been identified to have a high level of priority outside of our association's regular day-to-day operations. It establishes clear-cut goals, strategies, and action steps that will enable the board, committee volunteers, and managing agent to complete initiatives that will pave the way for a bright future for our community. This plan has a three-year duration period. Homeowner input will be an important part of the decision-making process, and the board will maintain close oversight to ensure timely completion of planning work within the framework of the association's budget.

This plan will be periodically updated to provide information about project status and modifications that add or change its goals and strategies. All updates and changes are subject to approval by the Association's board of directors.

DEFINITIONS, ROLES, AND RESPONSIBILITIES

Forest Grove: A residential community consisting of 624 single-family homes located in suburban Bethesda Maryland.

Forest Grove Community Association: A nonprofit corporation that has been formed to maintain the community's commonly owned property, ensure that the original design concept for the community is not substantially altered, provide community services, and protect and preserve the community's property values.

Board of Directors: The elected homeowners who are responsible for management of the association's operations and governance of the community.

Managing Agent: The community association management company that has been retained to carry out the operations of the association and provide community services on behalf of the board of directors.

Standing Committees: Groups of appointed homeowners to whom the board has delegated specific ongoing responsibilities that are carried out for the benefit of the community. The association's current standing committees are the following:

- **Covenants Committee**
- **Finance and Budget Committee**
- **Grounds and Facilities Committee**
- **Communications and Website Committee**

Ad Hoc Committees: Committees that are formed to perform a specific task that are dissolved after that task has been completed.

COMMUNITY VISION STATEMENT

Forest Grove is a community with a timeless aesthetic appearance that blends in with the natural beauty of its surrounding woodlands, creating a tranquil setting that will be preserved for years to come. This setting will promote an inclusive environment where neighbors can come together to enjoy life in a place that they can be proud to call home.

ASSOCIATION MISSION STATEMENT

The Forest Grove Community Association will serve the best interests of the general membership through efficient management of association operations, excellent stewardship of its finances, and superior maintenance of the community's infrastructure in order to preserve homeowner property values and achieve the community's vision for the future.

MASTER PLAN

STRENGTHS, WEAKNESSES, OPPORTUNITIES, AND THREATS

Utilizing data from our 2011 community survey, the Forest Grove Board of Directors and planning volunteers performed a SWOT analysis that identified and listed the association and community's most significant strengths, weaknesses, opportunities, and threats. The information in this comprehensive assessment was used to develop the 2011 strategic plan's goals and strategies.

Association and Community Strengths:
- Beautiful wooded neighborhood with large lots and attractive stately homes that blend in with the surrounding forest.
- Miles of paved walkways in the community's wooded areas.
- Forest Grove is a relatively private neighborhood.
- The central community clubhouse and recreation facilities.
- Strong management company. Helpful responsive staff.
- Smooth-running day-to-day association operations.
- Low-assessment payment delinquency.
- The association's financial condition is healthy.
- The landscaping company does an adequate job.

Association and Community Weaknesses:
- Weak board communications do not engage homeowners.
- Weak and underutilized association website.
- The association's volunteer base lacks motivation. Insufficient number of volunteers to handle committee workload.
- Board and committee members need training. Board needs to clarify and reinforce association-operating policies.

- Weak covenants program. Too many covenant violations, including a lack of home maintenance, failure to mow lawns and maintain landscape beds, and failure to comply with home exterior color guidelines (changes in trim colors from natural earth tone colors to bright primary and pastel colors).
- The asphalt clubhouse parking lot and woodlands walking paths are in in poor condition.
- Common area landscape beds need to be replaced.
- Weak signage. Main entrance to the community, clubhouse, and community villages are not impressive or inviting.
- Shabby clubhouse interior and outdated exercise equipment.

Opportunities That Could Have a Positive Impact on the Community and the Association's Ability to Conduct Business:

- A number of homeowners have indicated that they would be willing to volunteer for association committees.
- Pending state legislation may support stronger community association assessment collection rights.

Threats That Could Have a Negative Impact on the Community or Impede the Association's Ability to Conduct Business:

- The nationwide financial crisis may result in increased association assessment payment delinquency.
- Increasing competition from new housing developments in the area may have a negative impact on Forest Grove home values.
- The development of strip shopping centers in the area may have a negative impact on traffic around our community.
- Redistricting of school boundaries could have a negative impact on families with children in our community.

MASTER PLAN

GOALS, STATEGIES, AND ACTION STEPS

GOAL 1: Improve association communications.
- **Strategy:** Increase use of electronic communications to inform residents about association business and operations.
  - **Action Step:** Review, evaluate, and modify tracking procedures for major association projects that can be used to provide information for board communications to the community.
    - **Responsible Volunteer(s):** Board and Management
    - **Target Completion Date:** October 30, 2011
    - **Status:** Management has reviewed procedures and is drafting a procedural memo for board review and approval at the October board meeting.
  - **Action Step:** Establish an information distribution calendar and commence regular distribution of communitywide e-mail blasts covering general association operations and the status of pending and active projects.
    - **Responsible Volunteer(s):** Board and Management
    - **Target Completion Date:** October 30, 2011
    - **Status:** Management has completed the calendar and submitted it to the board for approval at the October board meeting.
  - **Action Step:** Institute a "Weekly News Flash" that the association office can send to homeowners at the end of each week in order to provide brief updates about routine association business and association rules reminders.
    - **Responsible Volunteer(s):** Board and Management
    - **Target Completion Date:** August 30, 2011

- **Status:** Action step completed. Weekly News Flashes were implement on August 19, 2011.
- **Strategy:** Create and distribute a quarterly community and association news magazine.
  - **Action Step:** Establish a relationship with a local magazine publisher that will publish a quarterly full-color news magazine at their own expense in exchange for community distribution and advertising rights.
    - **Responsible Volunteer(s):** Communications and Website Committee
    - **Target Completion Date:** November 30, 2011
    - **Status:** The committee is in the process of meeting with prospective service providers. Recommendations for a service provider will be made at the November board meeting.
  - **Action Step:** Work with the publisher to develop a quality magazine with a professional design format.
    - **Responsible Volunteer(s):** Communications and Website Committee
    - **Target Completion Date:** April 30, 2012
    - **Status:** Action pending. Design concept work will commence upon approval of a qualified service provider. It is anticipated that the magazine's design and content format will be completed by the end of the first quarter 2012. The design and content format will be submitted for approval at the April 2012 board meeting.
  - **Action Step:** Establish and maintain a pool of community and association volunteer contributors who will regularly submit articles of interest for publication.
    - **Responsible Volunteer(s):** Communications and Website Committee
    - **Target Completion Date:** December 30, 2011
    - **Status:** The committee is in the process of speaking with community residents, local professionals, and businesses owners who might be willing to contribute articles on a regular

MASTER PLAN

basis. A completed list of contributors will be presented at the December board meeting.
- **Action Step:** Launch publication and delivery.
  - **Responsible Volunteer(s):** Communications and Website Committee
  - **Target Completion Date:** June 30, 2012
  - **Status:** A preliminary launch schedule has been developed. The committee will begin to solicit and stockpile magazine articles in January 2012. Management will review articles to ensure that they are suitable for publication. It will be the publisher's responsibility to approach potential advertisers and sell ad space within the same time frame. The first quarterly magazine is tentatively scheduled for publication and delivery in June 2012.
- **Strategy:** Hold quarterly town hall meetings to facilitate open discussion between board members and homeowners outside of the structured environment of the board's regular monthly meetings.
  - **Action Step:** Determine if quarterly town hall meetings can be held in the same location as the annual meeting to ensure that it can accommodate a sufficient number of homeowners, develop an agenda that promotes open discussion, and initiate quarterly meetings.
    - **Responsible Volunteer(s):** Management
    - **Target Completion Date:** October 30, 2011
    - **Status:** Action step completed. An agenda format has been developed and approved by the board. Meetings will be held at the local library. The first quarterly town hall meeting is scheduled for October 18, 2011.

GOAL 2: Rebrand and modernize the association's image.
- **Strategy:** Create a distinctive logo that embodies our community's image and core values.

- **Action Step:** Contract with a local marketing company; obtain multiple logo options that are acceptable to the board. Conduct a "Pick a Logo" survey and poll homeowners to determine which of those logos are the most widely accepted by the community. Obtain final board approval of a logo based upon community polling data.
    - **Responsible Volunteer(s):** Communications and Website Committee
    - **Target Completion Date:** December 30, 2011
    - **Status:** A logo design schedule has been established. Based upon committee recommendation, a marketing company was approved by the board at the September 2011 board meeting. It is anticipated that logo options will be designed and presented to the board at its November 2011 meeting. A "Pick a Logo" poll will be sent to the community by mid-December. The results of the poll will be submitted to the board for final approval at its January 2012 meeting.
- **Strategy:** Develop and build a new website with an inviting and contemporary image that simplifies online homeowner access to association information, reduces costs through greater reliance on electronic communications, and enhances productivity by enabling staff to easily create and manage site content.
    - **Action Step:** Establish an internal Website Design Team consisting of qualified association volunteers, including Communications and Website Committee members, management staff, and community volunteers that have e-commerce marketing experience.
        - **Responsible Volunteer(s):** Communications and Website Committee and Management
        - **Target Completion Date:** October 30, 2011
        - **Status:** Prospective Website Design Team members have been identified and recruited.

MASTER PLAN

Approval of team members will be requested at the October board meeting.
- **Action Step:** Contract with a software service provider that specializes in community association website systems that can provide software that will enable the association to design and build its new customized website and e-mail blast program.
  - **Responsible Volunteer(s):** Website Design Team
  - **Target Completion Date:** March 30, 2012
  - **Status:** The design team is in the process of developing a request for performance (RFP). Anticipated completion date is November 30, 2011. Board approval of the RFP will be requested at the January 2012 board meeting. Upon approval, the committee will begin to prospect for qualified service providers. Candidates will be vetted, and a recommendation for a service provider will be made at the March 2012 board meeting.
- **Action Step:** Design and build the new website.
  - **Responsible Volunteer(s):** Website Design Team
  - **Target Completion Date:** July 30, 2012
  - **Status:** The design team will begin work once a qualified service provider has been identified and approved by the board.
- **Action Step:** Have the service provider cross-train the management staff and committee volunteers to ensure that the association has sufficient resources with the ability to manage the new website.
  - **Responsible Volunteer(s):** Website Design Team and Software Service Provider
  - **Target Completion Date:** August 30, 2012
  - **Status:** The Design Team will begin work once the website has been designed and built. It is anticipated that staff and committee training will take sixty days.

- **Action Step:** Transfer data, homeowner e-mail contact information, key association documents, and historical information from the old website to the new site.
  - **Responsible Volunteer(s):** Management
  - **Target Completion Date:** August 30, 2012
  - **Status:** Management staff will begin the transfer process after training has been completed. It is anticipated that the transfer can be completed within five working days.
- **Action Step:** Test the new website before live launch to ensure that the software functions properly, site speeds meet expectations, site navigation is simple and easy to use, data and information have successfully been transferred, and that e-mail blast and communication systems are operating in accordance with planned specifications.
  - **Responsible Volunteer(s):** Management
  - **Target Completion Date:** November 30, 2012
  - **Status:** Management staff will begin systems testing once the website has been built. It is anticipated that the association will run dual systems for ninety days to ensure that the new system functions properly prior to shut down of the old system.
- **Action Step:** Notify the community about the new website's launch date. Provide access information to ensure that all homeowners know how to locate the site in the Internet. Launch the site.
  - **Responsible Volunteer(s):** Management
  - **Target Completion Date:** December 15, 2012
  - **Status:** Based upon input from internal resources familiar with website design, a nine-month design, development, and

testing schedule has been recommended. Specific target dates for this work will be established once a qualified service provider has been identified and approved by the board.

GOAL 3: Develop a board and committee-training program that clarifies and reinforces compliance with the association's volunteer operating policies and procedures.

- **Strategy:** Establish a board of directors ad hoc committee that will work with management and legal counsel to evaluate and revise the Forest Grove Community Association Volunteer Handbook and ensure that it covers current volunteer policies and operating procedures.
  - **Action Step:** Establish the committee and have it work with management to review and update the handbook.
    - **Responsible Volunteer(s):** Board and Management
    - **Target Completion Date:** September 30, 2011
    - **Status:** Action step completed. The ad hoc committee has completed review and revised the volunteer handbook. Revisions were reviewed by legal counsel and approved by the board at its September meeting.
- **Strategy:** Have the ad hoc committee and management develop and commence training for board and committee members.
  - **Action Step:** Utilize the revised handbook to develop training material and presentations.
    - **Responsible Volunteer(s):** Board and Management
    - **Target Completion Date:** October 30, 2011

- **Status:** Action step completed. The first annual training session is scheduled for November 15, 2011.

GOAL 4: Evaluate and enhance the association's committee infrastructure. Increase the size of the volunteer base to improve productivity.
- **Strategy:** Review, evaluate, and modify committee charters to better reflect committee roles and responsibilities.
  - **Action Step:** Have committee chairs meet with their committees to develop recommendations for charter revisions.
    - **Responsible Volunteer(s):** Committee Chairs
    - **Target Completion Date:** December 30, 2011
    - **Status:** Committee chairs have scheduled special committee meetings with management to review their charters. Dates for review and completion of recommendations will vary based upon committee workloads.
  - **Action Step:** Pursuant to final review of committee recommendations, the board of directors will make final revisions to ensure that committee charters better reflect their responsibilities and authority to perform required work functions.
    - **Responsible Volunteer(s):** Board of Directors
    - **Target Completion Date:** March 2012
    - **Status:** The board will commence review of charters upon receipt of all committee recommendations.
- **Strategy:** Expand the volunteer base to enhance committee productivity.

MASTER PLAN

- **Action Step:** Increase the number of members for each committee to seven regular members and two alternate members.
  - **Responsible Volunteer(s):** Board of Directors
  - **Target Completion Date:** March 2012
  - **Status:** Charter revisions will include this change. The number of members for each committee will automatically be approved along with each committee's general charter revisions.
- **Strategy:** Implement a robust volunteer recruitment program to fill newly created vacancies and reduce total committee vacancies to 10% of the total volunteer base.
  - **Action Step:** Invite homeowners who have expressed interest in serving as volunteers to apply for committee membership.
    - **Responsible Volunteer(s):** Board of Directors
    - **Target Completion Date:** October 30, 2011
    - **Status:** All interested residents have been contacted. Committees are in the process of meeting with and vetting prospective candidates.
  - **Action Step:** Initiate monthly volunteer recruitment e-mail blasts and hold periodic committee "meet and greet" social gatherings with volunteer prospects.
    - **Responsible Volunteer(s):** Board, Committees, and Management
    - **Target Completion Date:** Activity will be ongoing.
    - **Status:** The board approved a recommended e-mail draft at its September meeting. Monthly recruitment e-mails will commence

in October 2011. Recruitment efforts will be ongoing to fill current and new vacancies on an as-needed basis.

GOAL 5: Enhance common area landscaping and strengthen the association's grounds maintenance procedures.

- **Strategy:** Refresh common area landscaping. Clear and replace weak and dead landscaping in common area landscape beds. Upgrade weak landscape stock with stronger drought resistant plant, bush, and tree species.
  - **Action Step:** Conduct a landscape inventory to identify missing, weak, and dead plants, bushes, and trees.
    - **Responsible Volunteer(s):** Grounds and Facilities Committee and Management
    - **Target Completion Date:** September 30, 2011
    - **Status:** Action step completed. A comprehensive replacement inventory has been established and is ready for distribution to landscape vendors.
  - **Action Step:** Obtain and vet three landscape bids. Ensure that sufficient reserve funds are available to complete all work. Develop a project plan and obtain board approval to proceed with the project.
    - **Responsible Volunteer(s):** Grounds and Facilities Committee and Finance and Budget Committee
    - **Target Completion Date:** December 30, 2011
    - **Status:** The committees are in the process of sourcing and vetting landscape bids. Upon determination of the winning bid, an analysis will be done to determine the impact of

MASTER PLAN

the project on the association's repair and replacement reserves. A complete project plan will be submitted for approval at the board's December 2011 meeting.

- **Action Step:** Remove weak and dead plants, bushes, and trees from landscape beds. Install new landscaping. Monitor progress to ensure that the work is completed in accordance with project's job specifications and schedule.
  - **Responsible Volunteer(s):** Grounds and Facilities Committee
  - **Target Completion Date:** October 30, 2012
  - **Status:** The project will be completed in two phases. The first phase will be completed during the 2012 spring planting season. The second phase will be completed during the 2012 fall planting season.
- **Action Step:** Increase bed-mulching and grass-fertilizing from one to two times per year.
  - **Responsible Volunteer(s):** Management
  - **Target Completion Date:** Activity will be ongoing.
  - **Status:** Action step completed. The operating budget will be adjusted for 2012 to cover the cost of additional mulching. Mulching will be done in the spring and fall of each year.
- **Strategy:** Develop an effective landscape-monitoring program.
  - **Action Step:** Begin monthly inspections to ensure that that the landscape company performs in accordance with the terms of its contract and that landscape deficiencies are addressed on a timely basis.
    - **Responsible Volunteer(s):** Grounds and Facilities Committee and Management

- **Target Completion Date:** September 30, 2011
- **Status:** Action step completed. Monthly inspections commenced in September 2011.
- **Action Step:** Initiate and conduct monthly sprinkler system inspections to ensure that breaks in lines, missing sprinkler heads, and defective sprinkler lines and equipment are repaired on a timely basis.
  - **Responsible Volunteer(s):** Management
  - **Target Completion Date:** September 30, 2011
  - **Status:** Action step completed. The sprinkler system service provider has been tasked to conduct monthly inspections commencing September 2011. The 2012 budget has been adjusted to cover the cost of the additional service.

GOAL 6: Address and correct community facilities deficiencies.

- **Strategy:** Redecorate and refurbish the interior of the community clubhouse.
  - **Action Step:** Establish a design team consisting of members of the Grounds and Facilities Committee, board members, and a paid independent interior design consultant. Charge the team with the responsibility to develop a complete decorating plan for the clubhouse, including its common areas, meeting rooms, fitness center, association offices, and restrooms.
    - **Responsible Volunteer(s):** Board of Directors and Grounds and Facilities Committee
    - **Target Completion Date:** November 30, 2011

MASTER PLAN

- **Status:** Internal association team members have been identified. Design consultants are being sourced and interviewed. Vetting of a qualified consultant will be completed by the end of October 2011. The recommended consultant will be submitted for board approval at its November 2011 meeting.
- **Action Step:** Develop a design plan, including paint colors, wallpaper, flooring, light fixtures, window coverings, furniture, artwork, and accessories.
  - **Responsible Volunteer(s):** Design Team
  - **Target Completion Date:** March 30, 2012
  - **Status:** Work will commence in December 2011 subject to board approval of the design consultant.
- **Action Step:** Establish a budget, funding plan, and project timeline. Confirm that sufficient reserve funds are available to complete the project.
  - **Responsible Volunteer(s):** Design Team and Finance and Budget Committee
  - **Target Completion Date:** May 30, 2012
  - **Status:** Financial work and timeline development will commence upon completion of the design plan in March 2012.
- **Action Step:** Hold a town hall meeting to introduce the design plans to the community.
  - **Responsible Volunteer(s):** Design Team
  - **Target Completion Date:** July 30, 2012
  - **Status:** Action pending. A town hall meeting will be scheduled once the design plan, budget, and project timeline have been developed.
- **Action Step:** Implement the refurbishing project.
  - **Responsible Volunteer(s):** Design Team

- **Target Completion Date:** August 30, 2012
- **Status:** Subject to community feedback, the final plan will be submitted for approval at the August 2012 board meeting. Project work will begin at the beginning of the following month.
- **Action Step:** Monitor progress to ensure that the project is completed in accordance with the plan's specifications and schedule.
  - **Responsible Volunteer(s):** Design Team, Finance and Budget Committee, and Management
  - **Target Completion Date:** March 2013
  - **Status:** Inspections and progress monitoring will begin as soon as the project is initiated. It is anticipated that once work has commenced, work can be completed within six months.
- **Strategy:** Inspect fitness and workout equipment. Repair or replace defective and worn-out equipment.
  - **Action Step:** Have a qualified contractor inspect all exercise equipment. Determine which machines can be salvaged and which machines need to be replaced.
    - **Responsible Volunteer(s):** Design Team
    - **Target Completion Date:** October 30, 2011
    - **Status:** A qualified inspector has been identified. Inspections have been scheduled for the first week in October 2011.
  - **Action Step:** Establish a budget. Repair salvageable equipment, and replace the equipment that cannot be salvaged.
    - **Responsible Volunteer(s):** Design Team and Finance and Budget Committee
    - **Target Completion Date:** March 30, 2012

- **Status:** A budget will be developed by the end of December 2011. Subject to confirmation of the availability of funds, a final project plan will be submitted to the board for approval at its January 2012 meeting. It is anticipated that repair and replacement work can be completed by the end of the first quarter 2012.
- **Strategy:** Develop a plan for upgraded entrance features and community signs that will substantially enhance the appearance of the main entrance to the community, clubhouse, and various residential villages. The design concept will optimize the use of the community's new logo and branding image and incorporate the use of stone monuments with wrought iron accents, upscale carriage lighting, and upgraded landscaping.
  - **Action Step:** Hire a landscape and hardscape designer.
    - **Responsible Volunteer(s):** Grounds and Facilities Committee
    - **Target Completion Date:** January 30, 2012
    - **Status:** The committee is in the process of interviewing landscape architects. It is anticipated that it will take ninety days to identify a qualified service provider, negotiate a design contract, and obtain board approval to proceed with concept development.
  - **Action Step:** Develop a design plan and request for proposal (RFP) that sets forth construction and landscape specifications, county permit requirements for hardscape construction and electrical work, and bid prices.
    - **Responsible Volunteer(s):** Grounds and Facilities Committee and Finance and Budget Committee
    - **Target Completion Date:** May 2012

- **Status:** Once the services of an architect are secured, it is anticipated that it will take four months to develop a design plan and RFP.
- **Action Step:** Obtain three acceptable RFP responses. Vet the contractors, bid prices, and proposed construction schedules to ensure that they meet the RFP's requirements.
  - **Responsible Volunteer(s):** Grounds and Facilities Committee and Finance and Budget Committee
  - **Target Completion Date:** September 30, 2012
  - **Status:** Once responses have been received, it is anticipated that it will take sixty days to vet the contractors and their bid proposals.
- **Action Step:** Establish a budget, funding plan, and project timeline. Confirm that sufficient reserve funds are available to complete the project. Submit the final plan to the board for approval.
  - **Responsible Volunteer(s):** Grounds and Facilities Committee
  - **Target Completion Date:** December 30, 2012
  - **Status:** Once a final bid proposal is identified, it is anticipated that it will take ninety days to establish the final project plan and obtain board approval to proceed with work. The final plan will be submitted for approval at the December 2012 board meeting.
- **Action Step:** Commence construction and landscape work. Monitor progress to ensure that the project is completed within the required time frame and within budget.
  - **Responsible Volunteer(s):** Grounds and Facilities Committee
  - **Target Completion Date:** October 30, 2013
  - **Status:** It is anticipated that work will commence in late spring 2013; hardscape construction will be competed within ninety

MASTER PLAN

days, followed by landscape installation during the fall planting season.
- **Strategy:** Repair or replace the asphalt parking lot at the central clubhouse and recreation facility and the asphalt walking paths in the community's wooded areas.
  - **Action Step:** Secure the services of a qualified engineer to measure the parking lot and walking paths and provide project specifications.
    - **Responsible Volunteer(s):** Grounds and Facilities Committee
    - **Target Completion Date:** October 30, 2011
    - **Status:** A qualified engineer has been identified and approved by the board. Measurement work is in progress.
  - **Action Step:** Develop a request for proposal (RFP) based upon the engineer's project specifications.
    - **Responsible Volunteer(s):** Grounds and Facilities Committee and Finance and Budget Committee
    - **Target Completion Date:** January 30, 2012
    - **Status:** Once final engineering specifications have been received, it is anticipated that it will take ninety days to develop an RFP.
  - **Action Step:** Obtain three RFP responses. Vet contractor work plans and bid prices to ensure that they meet the RFP's requirements.
    - **Responsible Volunteer(s):** Grounds and Facilities Committee and Finance and Budget Committee
    - **Target Completion Date:** April 30, 2012
    - **Status:** Once RFP responses have been received, it is anticipated that it will take sixty days to vet the contractors and their bid proposals.
  - **Action Step:** Establish a budget, funding plan, and project timeline. Confirm that sufficient

reserve funds are available to complete the project. Submit the final plan to the board for approval.
- **Responsible Volunteer(s):** Grounds and Facilities Committee and Finance and Budget Committee
- **Target Completion Date:** July 30, 2012
- **Status:** Once a final bid proposal has been identified, it is anticipated that it will take ninety days to establish the final project plan and obtain board approval to proceed with work. The finished plan will be submitted to the board for approval at its July 2012 meeting.

- **Action Step:** Implement the project plan in phases that take into account seasonal weather conditions. Monitor progress to ensure that each phase of the project is completed on time and within budget.
  - **Responsible Volunteer(s):** Grounds and Facilities Committee
  - **Target Completion Date:** August 30, 2014
  - **Status:** Work will be done during the summer season in three phases: (1) clubhouse parking lot to be completed by August 30, 2012; (2) north and east walking paths to be completed by August 30, 2013; and (3) south and west walking paths to be completed by August 30, 2014.

GOAL 7: Strengthen the association's covenants program.
- **Strategy:** Review and update the association's architectural design guidelines, and revise covenants inspection and enforcement procedures in order to enhance program productivity.
  - **Action Step:** Review and update the covenants guidelines to ensure that they clearly and accurately reflect the association's current policies.

MASTER PLAN

- **Responsible Volunteer(s):** Covenants Committee, Management, and Legal Counsel
- **Target Completion Date:** November 30, 2011
- **Status:** Guidelines review has been completed. Revisions will be recommended, distributed to the community for comment, and then submitted to the board for approval in accordance with requirements set forth in the association's governing documents.

• **Action Step:** Establish procedures that facilitate annual Covenants Committee and board review of the architectural design guidelines to ensure that recommended changes are made within the framework of the association's governing documents and applicable state law. Ensure that these procedures call for review and approval of all changes by the association's legal counsel.
- **Responsible Volunteer(s):** Covenants Committee and Management
- **Target Completion Date:** September 30, 2011
- **Status:** Action step completed. The new procedures were submitted and approved by the board at its September 2011 meeting.

• **Action Step:** Review enforcement policies and procedures with management and legal counsel to ensure that they are strong enough to facilitate resolution of cited violations in accordance with the association's governing documents, current policies, and applicable state and federal law.
- **Responsible Volunteer(s):** Covenants Committee and Management
- **Target Completion Date:** October 30, 2011
- **Status:** A preliminary review has been completed. Recommendations have been submitted to legal counsel for review and comment. It is anticipated that a final draft will

be submitted to the board for approval at its October meeting.
- **Strategy:** Strengthen the covenants inspection process.
  - **Action Step:** Move from monthly drive-by inspections to semiannual comprehensive inspections that will cover all exterior elements of each house and lot.
    - **Responsible Volunteer(s):** Covenants Committee and Management
    - **Target Completion Date:** September 30, 2011
    - **Status:** Action step completed. Semiannual comprehensive inspections will commence in October 2011.
  - **Action Step:** Add a full-time covenants inspector to the management staff to support the increased property inspection workload.
    - **Responsible Volunteer(s):** Board and Management
    - **Target Completion Date:** October 30, 2011
    - **Status:** Candidates for the position have been identified. A final decision and employment offer will be made in October 2011.
  - **Action Step:** Establish appropriate board and Covenants Committee oversight procedures to ensure that the management company is conducting inspections in accordance with board directives. Procedures will include monitoring of management and legal counsel violations resolution activity reports.
    - **Responsible Volunteer(s):** Covenants Committee and Management
    - **Target Completion Date:** October 30, 2011
    - **Status:** Action step completed. Procedures have been established. Monitoring will

begin in conjunction with the first semiannual comprehensive inspection that will be conducted in October 2011.
- **Strategy**: Implement a homeowner education program that reinforces the importance of maintaining the original aesthetic vision for homes in the community, typical maintenance violations that can be easily avoided, efforts that are being taken to strengthen enforcement, and the consequences for failure to comply with the association's architectural guidelines and covenants.
  - **Action Step:** Develop education material, including stock e-mail blasts and association news magazine articles.
    - **Responsible Volunteer(s):** Covenants Committee, Management, and Board of Directors
    - **Target Completion Date:** December 30, 2011
    - **Status:** Program development began in September 2011. It is anticipated that work will be completed during the last quarter of 2011.
  - **Action Step:** Develop a quarterly distribution schedule.
    - **Responsible Volunteer(s):** Covenants Committee and Management
    - **Target Completion Date:** December 30, 2011
    - **Status:** Work is in progress and will be completed in conjunction with the development of the program's education material.

COMMUNICATIONS AND FEEDBACK

The board of directors will disseminate communitywide quarterly planning status updates and special notices when major project milestones have been reached. Homeowners will be encouraged to provide feedback about planning initiatives and progress. Information will be disseminated by e-mail blast and the association's website. The board will also engage in ongoing dialogue with committee volunteers and homeowners about planning activity at its regular monthly meetings, the annual meeting, and at periodic town hall meetings. Surveys may also be conducted to obtain homeowner input that will supplement research and due diligence prior to initiating new plan initiatives.

PROJECT IMPLEMENTATION, PROGRESS MONITORING, AND PLAN MODIFICATION

The board of directors will task volunteers with the responsibility to develop and implement action steps that will be required to carry out the plan's various strategies. These actions steps shall not be initiated without a complete project and financial plan that has been approved by the board. To facilitate board oversight, volunteers will provide project activity reports at monthly board meetings that enable the board to monitor progress, address priorities, modify plan goals and strategies, and ensure that work is proceeding within the framework of the association's budget. Priorities and deadlines are subject to change, at the sole discretion of the board, based upon association needs, available volunteer resources, and budget considerations.

EPILOGUE

FOREST GROVE...2014

In early April 2014, I received an invitation to attend a lunch meeting at Forest Grove. The association was completing work on its 2011 strategic plan, and consideration was being given to launching another planning initiative. Board members were hoping to develop the new plan without outside professional assistance. They were anxious to get my opinion about their ability to handle the project on their own. It had been nearly three years since I last met with them. I was curious to hear about the results of their efforts and wanted to see the impact that their work had on the community.

Prior to our meeting, I reviewed the latest updated version of the 2011 plan and noted that it provided clear and complete project status information and activity dates. With the exception of a few well-thought-out modifications, most of the strategies had been carried out in accordance with the original plan, and more than 90% of its action steps had been completed. The remaining work was scheduled for completion within the next sixty days, at which time all the plan's goals would be fully achieved.

When I drove through the community before the meeting, it was evident that a lot of progress had been made. The small entry signs at the main entrance had been replaced with large signs emblazoned with the association's rebranded logos on impressive stone and wood monuments that were surrounded by lush landscaping. This theme was repeated at the entries to the community's different villages and the central clubhouse and recreation facility. The crumbling walking paths and clubhouse parking lot had been resurfaced with new asphalt. Landscaping in the association's common areas was well cared for and attractive. A positive trend had developed as many homeowners took on a renewed interest in improving the landscaping around their own homes. Violations related to paint colors on trim, shutters, and doors that did not meet the community's earth-tone color criteria had been cured. Houses with bright primary or pastel colors no longer "stood out," enabling the community's homes to blend in with the surrounding forest and natural environment. Forest Grove's stately homes and oversize lots were now showcased by attractive and well-maintained streetscapes.

Before lunch the board members took me on a tour of the clubhouse. The interior was freshly painted, and new tile floors had been installed throughout the building. New furnishings, draperies, light fixtures, artwork, and accessories created an elegant contemporary setting, and the association offices had been refurbished, resulting in a professional work environment. The workout facility and restrooms had been completely redone with durable semigloss paint, contemporary nonslip floor tiles, and sleek modern plumbing fixtures. The pool deck had been pressure cleaned and was filled with new chaise lounges, patio tables, and umbrellas. It was clear that the board had accomplished its objective to create a pleasant and inviting central meeting place for the community.

Lunch conversation was enlightening. With good reason, the board was proud of what the association had accomplished. I was dealing with the same president and directors that I met with in 2011, but unlike our first meeting that began with a cautious and defensive tone, this conversation was extremely positive. The board members had a good story to share. They knew that there was a vast change in the appearance of their community that would no doubt have a positive impact on property values, but the changes that resulted from their work went far beyond the community's appearance. Prior to the

MASTER PLAN

planning initiative, association operations might have been adequate, but things needed to get better, so the board took the operation to a higher level. The intrinsic value of proactive clear communications, strong leadership, and the board's willingness to reach out to homeowners and listen to what they had to say could not be quantified. Nonetheless, there had been a noticeable change for the better in the board's relationship with the community. Homeowners recognized and appreciated the results of the association's hard work. The size of the volunteer base had increased to a level that significantly enhanced productivity. Well-motivated committee members and management clearly understood their responsibilities and efficiently went about their work with positive attitudes. There was now a spirit of cooperation that made the association's job much easier than it had been in the past.

The board members had learned a lot about planning, leadership, and communications. That knowledge was used to carry out a plan that would benefit Forest Grove for years to come. It was time for me to give my opinion about their ability to move ahead without professional assistance and guidance. I used a famous quote to emphasize my point.

> There is no deodorant like success.
>
> —Elizabeth Taylor
> Life Magazine, December 18, 1964

My answer was yes…they now had the ability and confidence to do the job. It was time for them to move ahead on their own.

REFERENCES

Chapter 1

Community Associations Institute. *Community Associations in the United States*. Accessed March 12, 2019. https://www.caionline.org/AboutCommunityAssociations/Pages/StatisticalInformation.

Duncan, Dr. R., (2012). *Change Friendly Leadership*. United States: Maxwell Stone Publishing.

Kouzes, J. & Posner, B. (2010). *The Truth About Leadership*. San Francisco, CA: Josey-Bass.

National Association of Housing Cooperatives. Buying into a Housing Cooperative. Accessed March 27, 2019. https://coophousing.org/resources/owning-a-housing cooperative/buying-into-a-housing- cooperative/#paragraph1.

Pyhrr, S., Cooper, J., Wofford, L., Kapplin, S. & Lapides, P. (1989). *Real Estate Investment 2nd Edition*, New York, NY: John Wiley & Sons.

Wikipedia-The Free Encyclopedia. *Housing Cooperatives*. Accesssed February 14, 2019. https://en.wikipedia.org/wiki/Housing_Cooperative.

Chapter 2

Burke, R. & Barron, S. (2014). *Project Management Leadership*. United Kingdom: John Wiley & Sons.

Foundation for Community Association Research. *Best Practices Report #3, Strategic Planning*. Accessed July 15, 2019. https://foundation.caionline.org/wp-content/uploads/2017/06/bpsstrategic.pdf.

Grensig-Pophal, L. (2011). *The Complete Idiots Guide to Strategic Planning*. New York, NY: Penguin Group.

Koegel, T. (2007). *The Exceptional Presenter*. Austin Texas: Greenleaf Book Group Press.

Robert III, H., Honemann, D. & Balch T. (2011). *Robert's Rules of Order Revised 11th Edition*. Philadelphia, PA: Da Capo Press.

Chapter 3

Iacocca, L. With Novak, W. (1984). *Iacocca, An Autobiography*. New York, NY: Bantam Books.

McLeod, S. *What's the Difference Between Qualitative and Quantitative Research? Simply Psychology*. Accessed June 8, 2019. https://www.simplypsychology.org/qualitative-quantitative.html.

Wikipedia-The Free Encyclopedia. *Proactive Communications*, Accessed June 18, 2019. https://en.wikipedia.org/wiki/Proactive_communications.

Chapter 4

Grensig-Pophal, L. (2011). *The Complete Idiots Guide to Strategic Planning*. New York, NY: Penguin Group.

Wikipedia-The Free Encyclopedia. *Business Plan*. Accessed August 10, 2019. https: //en.wikepedia.org/wiki/Business_plan.

ABOUT THE AUTHOR

Alan Robbins has had a distinguished thirty-year commercial banking career holding senior management positions and serving on the boards of major financial institutions and industry trade organizations. He is a past president of the Mortgage Bankers Association of Florida and a recipient of its Brown L. Whatley Award for meritorious services to Florida's mortgage banking industry. As an advocate for fair lending initiatives, he has been recognized by the Department of Housing and Urban Development for his contributions to the nation's housing industry. He is currently a member of Virginia's Loudoun County Housing Advisory Board.

Robbins has also served as marketing and membership director of the Washington Metropolitan Chapter of the Community Associations Institute, where he led the marketing and membership efforts for the association in Maryland, Virginia, and the District of Colombia, as it provided services to the chapter's 2,500 members, including professional community association managers and community volunteers from more than 800 associations representing 260,000 households.

Mr. Robbins is a graduate of Nova Southeastern University, where he received his Master's in Business Administration degree in Real Estate Development and Management. He has served on the boards of small- and large-scale homeowners associations and provided strategic planning consulting services and financial guidance to community associations, real estate developers, and property management companies in Florida and Virginia. His extensive background has provided him with unique perspectives that enable him to pave the way to effective board governance, successful associations, and stronger communities.

www.ingramcontent.com/pod-product-compliance
Lightning Source LLC
Chambersburg PA
CBHW030904180526
45163CB00004B/1702